FIRST STEPS TO DIS- COVERING GOD

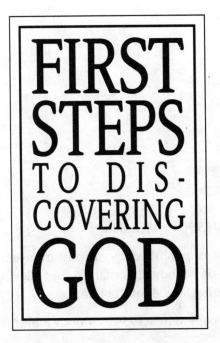

FIRST STEPS TO DIS-COVERING GOD

PRESENTED TO

_____

_____

_____

FROM

_____

_____

_____

MERIDIAN
PUBLICATIONS

Contents

Preface

To begin to find the Christian life in all its fullness, we must first grasp all that is promised to us and required of us by God's Word and begin to apply it.

First Steps to Discovering God was initially developed and taught at Moody Bible Institute in Chicago. For more than forty years it has been part of a Bible correspondence course for the External Studies Division of Moody Bible Institute.

Now, for the first time, this incisive and insightful study is available for personal or group Bible study to help believers apply the principles of God's Word and come to enjoy the Christian life as God intended it.

—The Publisher

Introduction

Sing to the LORD, bless His name;
Proclaim the good news of His salvation
from day to day (Psalm 96:2 NKJV).

But what is the good news of salvation? Before we can proclaim it we must know what it is. This book provides the answer. Designed to be biblical, specific, and practical, it will also teach you how to apply the truth of the good news to your own life.

This book and others in the *Christian Life Application* series provide study materials on the various aspects of living a full, rich Christian life. Meridian titles in addition to *First Steps to Discovering God* in the *Christian Life Application* series currently include:

First Steps to Knowing God's Will
First Steps for New Christians
First Steps to Understanding Your Bible

Additional titles in the *Christian Life Application* series are forthcoming.

Because these materials were initially used both as classroom and correspondence school texts, the style is that of a teacher—guiding, challenging, directing, stimulating, and raising questions as well as providing answers.

The content of this edition is taken from an adult credit course from the External Studies Division of Moody Bible Institute. For information on how you might take this and other courses for credit, write for a free catalog to:

Moody External Studies
Moody Bible Institute
820 N. La Salle
Chicago, IL 60610

1

A Wonderful Miracle

Do You Believe in Miracles?

George Muller was a drunkard and a rebel until a sudden, total, and revolutionary change took place in his life. He became instead a good and godly man, dedicated to the care, support, and education of thousands of orphan boys and girls. He was renowned for his remarkable and practical piety around the world.

A prominent surgeon, Professor Rendle Short, who lived in Muller's hometown of Bristol, England, said, "During the second half of the nineteenth century the life and example of George Muller of Bristol were mightily used of God to strengthen faith all around the world. I have heard my father say that through those years atheism in Bristol scarcely dared to raise its voice, knowing it would be instantly challenged."[1] What happened to George Muller to transform him so completely?

Jim Vaus was a gangster. In his book *Why I Quit Syndicated Crime*, he tells how, as an electronics expert, he worked with criminals and police simultaneously. Finally, he decided that crime paid best. Jim Vaus was reared in a Christian home and went to Sunday school and to a Bible institute. However, he became a gangster and was becoming prominent in the underworld when the same type of change that revolutionized George Muller transformed him as well. Jim Vaus paid his debt to society and became a dedicated Christian working to bring the same experience to youthful toughs in Harlem. What happened to Jim Vaus to change him from a criminal into a Christian?

Throughout the world today this same wonderful miracle is taking place, though unknown and unbelieved by the great majority of the people. Like every other true miracle, it cannot be explained by merely human knowledge; nor can it be detected or diagnosed by human devices. A doctor's instruments will not reveal how or when it happens. The best-trained scientists cannot record or explain what it is that takes place.

This miracle takes place constantly in the human realm. It happens to people of all cultures, of all nationalities, of all ages, and even of all religious backgrounds. And yet this statement should be qualified, because actually it is

---

1 Rendle Short, *The Rock Beneath* (London: InterVarsity Fellowship, 1955), 140.

found more frequently among the poor, the despised, and the outcasts than it is among the wise, the mighty, and the noble (1 Corinthians 1:26–29).

THE MIRACLE OF THE NEW BIRTH

What is this miracle that reaches into all strata of society with amazing and far-reaching results? It is the mysterious, divine, extraordinary event known as the *new birth*—or, as some prefer to call it—*conversion* or *salvation*.

It is called the *new birth* because it is the beginning of a new spiritual life, just as ordinary birth is the beginning of natural life (1 Peter 1: 23).

It is called *conversion* because it represents an about-face in one's life, a change from unbelief to faith (Matthew 18:3).

It is called *salvation* because it means the rescue of a person from the penalty and power of sin and also from even the presence of sin in the life to come (1 Peter 1:4–5).

WHAT IS THE NEW BIRTH?

The new birth is a *spiritual* occurrence. "That which is born of the Spirit is spirit" (John 3:6). By that is meant that it is not concerned primarily with the physical, visible part of a man's nature, namely, his body; but rather with his nonmaterial being, that is, his spirit and soul.

Then the new birth is distinctly a *supernatural* event. "Salvation is of the Lord" (Jonah 2:9). It cannot be produced by a man or by any group of men. It is not of blood—that is, it is not inherited; children of born-again parents are not automatically born again. It is not of the will; a man cannot experience conversion simply by wishing it to be so. It is not by persuasion. A minister or preacher, priest or rabbi, cannot bring about another's salvation, no matter how earnestly either one or the other may desire it (John 1:13).

The new birth is a *sovereign* act of God. Just as the wind blows where it wishes without asking man's permission, so God extends his gift of salvation to individuals without first consulting human governments, church officials, or any other person or group of persons (John 3:8).

The spiritual birth of a soul occurs *instantaneously*, although the events leading up to it may cover a period of months or even years. The first moment a person looks by faith to Jesus Christ and trusts him as Savior and Lord, he receives everlasting life (John 3:36).

THE NEW BIRTH VERSUS AN EMPTY PROFESSION

The new birth can be and often *is imitated.* Such spurious conversions may be referred to as "professions" or mere "reformations. " They often are based on nothing more than baptism, confirmation, church membership, or a religious rite or ceremony. But nothing short of salvation will give lasting peace to the soul or gain a person an entrance into heaven. Invariably, when a person has merely turned over a new leaf without experiencing the new birth, he later lapses into sinful ways more wicked than at first (Matthew 12:44–45). Thus, while conversion can be imitated, it cannot be duplicated. Only faith in Christ has permanence.

THE NEW BIRTH BY FAITH IN CHRIST ALONE

Testimonies from five Christians would reveal five different backgrounds; yet all are saved in exactly the same way.

In one sense, to be saved is a very simple matter. True faith in the Lord Jesus Christ is the key that unlocks God's treasurehouse (Acts 16:31). No other key will fit or bring the desired blessing (Acts 4:12).

Yet a person often makes it difficult. He says he cannot believe. Does he have the right kind or amount of faith? Will God really accept him if he trusts the Savior? And so with these and similar reasonings, arguments, and doubts, he obstructs his own pathway to eternal life.

THE FAR-REACHING RESULTS OF THE NEW BIRTH

Although we cannot explain the new birth, we certainly can see its results. In fact, it is the mightiest demonstration of power in the world today. For it is this awesome force that changes a persecuting Saul to a crusading Paul, that changes him spiritually from death to life, that changes him morally from darkness to light, that changes him practically from sin to holiness, and that changes his destiny from hell to heaven (Acts 9:1–9).

THE NEW BIRTH EXPLAINED IN THE BIBLE

The only reliable source of information about the new birth is the Holy Bible—God's revelation to humanity. The classic passage in the Scriptures on being born again is John 3:1–17.

A PERSONAL QUESTION

After reading these words from the lips of the Son of

God you must admit that the conclusion is inescapable—apart from the new birth there is no possibility of reaching heaven. And so every reader should seriously face the question that inevitably arises and persistently waits for an answer, "Have I ever been born again?"

WHY YOU MUST BE BORN AGAIN

The late Dr. R. A. Torrey told of a conversation with a physician in Kansas. The physician told Torrey how great an influence his mother had exerted on his life. "I have always lived up to her teachings morally," he said, "and I pride myself on the fact that while I was away in the medical institution, I kept myself morally clean. I do not profess to be a Christian, but I am a better man morally than any of the church members in this city."

"Doctor," replied Torrey, "I do not doubt you for an instant, but I want your attention. Unregeneracy is a state. You have not been regenerated [i.e., born again] have you?"

The physician replied, "No sir, I do not claim to be a regenerated man."

Dr. Torrey was standing by the side of the physician. He drew a square on the ground and said, "Doctor, let this square represent the state of Colorado. The summit of Pike's Peak is 14,110 feet above sea level. The altitude at the lowest point is 2,000 feet above sea level, and there are people in Colorado mines who are 3,000 feet below the lowest altitude of the state. Whether they are in the mines, on the lowest altitude, or on the summit of Pike's Peak, they are all in the state of Colorado.

"Now the state of unregeneracy is like that. Some men are always down below the surface in the underground villainy and terrible criminality of flagrant wickedness; others range about the surface, the lowest altitude in the state of unregeneracy, while you are on the summit of Mount Morality; but you are still in the state of unregeneracy."

The man looked at Dr. Torrey in amazement and then said without an argument, "You have knocked the props out from under me. I am with you." He then publicly confessed Jesus Christ as his personal Savior.

As you study this book I trust that you too will recognize your need to be born again.

2

*N*ew Life Needed

Why is the new birth necessary? Why did God ever have to devise such a plan for human beings?

The answer is found in a little three-letter word: S-I-N. It is the fact of SIN that caused God to devise salvation's plan. It is the existence of evil in the human heart that makes the new birth necessary. If people were holy, they would not need salvation.

A HOLY GOD VIEWS SIN

In discussing the subject of sin, it is of extreme importance to view it from God's standpoint rather than from our own.

God is holy (Isaiah 6:3). He is pure. He is good (Matthew 19:17). He is sin-hating (Romans 1:18). He is righteous

(Psalm 11:7). He is just (Isaiah 45:21). He is perfect (Psalm 18:30). We, on the other hand, are blinded by our own sins. We are prejudiced. We think of sin lightly. Thus one sin in God's sight is worse than a thousand sins in ours. Just as we can know a crooked line only by comparing it with a straight one, so we can see sin as it really is only by comparing it with God's absolute holiness.

In God's pure eyes, sin is anything less than perfection in thought, word, or deed. It means missing the mark. It is not only the act of doing wrong but includes also the failure to do what one knows to be right (James 4:17) and even the thought of foolishness (Proverbs 24:9). In order that we might know what sin is, God has given us two outstanding standards:

1. The Law, or Ten Commandments (Exodus 20:1–17)

These really demand absolute perfection. To follow them completely would mean sinlessness. They are therefore an expression of the glory of God—his utter holiness.

2. The Lord Jesus Christ

God's beloved Son was sinless. He knew no sin (2 Corinthians 5:21). He did no sin (1 Peter 2:22). There was no sin in him (1 John 3:5). The Gospels thus record the life story of a sinless person. In every way in which our lives fall short of his, we are sinners.

ALL HAVE SINNED

In God's holy light, all men are sinners. "For all have sinned and come short of the glory of God" (Romans 3:23).

First of all, we became sinners by *birth*. Adam, the father of the human race, sinned, and all his children were thereby sinners.

> By one man sin entered into the world, and death by sin; and so death passed upon all men, for that all have sinned (Romans 5:12).

When children are born into a family of poverty, they inherit this condition. So man is born into a sinful family and becomes possessor of a sinful nature with a definite inclination to sin (Psalm 58:3). It is easy for him to do wrong, and he must make a distinct effort to do right.

Then, we are sinners by *practice* (Ecclesiastes 7:20). Sin is our deliberate, personal choice. We like it. Some, it is true, are more outrageous and vicious sinners than others. Yet one sin proves one to be a sinner, and all have sinned.

Dr. Roland Q. Leavell of New Orleans tells the story of a college sophomore who came to see him. This sophomore was all the name sophomore implies (the word comes from two Greek words, *sophos,* meaning wise, and *moron,* meaning just what you think it does). This young man was a wise moron. He said to Dr. Leavell, "I would like to discuss Christianity on an intellectual basis. Don't tell me that I'm a sinner; that type of thinking went out with Noah's ark. Let's discuss it on an intellectual basis."

Dr. Leavell said, "Very well; will you allow me to lead the discussion?"

And this college sophomore, proving that he was a wise moron, said yes.

Dr. Leavell said, "Young man, what do you think about Wellhausen's documentary hypothesis concerning the authorship of the Pentateuch? Do you believe that *Aleph* wrote it, or *Beth, Gimel, Daleth, He,* or a combination of them?"

The sophomore said, "You know, I hadn't thought much about that."

Dr. Leavell said, "Young man, what is your attitude toward the parthenogenesis account of Christ?"

He said, "I don't believe I have an attitude in that direction."

Dr. Leavell said, "You know, of course, that the Old Testament for the most part was written in Hebrew. But there are certain Aramaic passages that appear in the Hebrew text and have a definite flavoring on the interpretation of the context. I'll take my Masoretic text and will read the Hebrew, and when I come to an Aramaic passage, I'll turn the Bible over to you, and you read it and tell me what the Aramaic means."

The boy said, "I'm afraid that would be Greek to me."

Dr. Leavell said, "What do you think of the ontological, the teleological, the anthropological, and the cosmological arguments for the existence of God?"

He said, "You know, I hadn't thought much about them."

Dr. Leavell said, "I'm going to ask you one more question on an intellectual basis, and if you can't answer that question because you can't understand it, then I'm going to ask you some questions which you can understand and I'm sure you can answer."

And the young man said, "Very well."

"Young man, what are your eschatological predilections; are they premillennarian, promillennarian, amillennarian or postmillennarian?"

The young man said, "I don't believe I have any."

Then Dr. Leavell said, "Young man, did you ever lie? You can understand that, can't you?"

The boy said, "Yes, I can understand it. I've told a few white lies, but not many black ones."

Dr. Leavell said, "In the eyes of God, there are no white lies; they are all black. Therefore in the eyes of God you're a liar. Young man, did you ever steal?"

"Well," he said, "when I was in high school I cheated on a few examinations."

Dr. Leavell said, "In the eyes of God, then, you are a thief. Young man, did you ever hate anybody?"

The young man said, "Well, just a few of my high school teachers."

"The Bible says hatred can amount to murder. Therefore in the eyes of God you are a murderer. Now, what does God see when he looks at you? First of all, he sees a liar; secondly, he sees a thief; and in the third place, he sees a murderer. Do you still believe that the doctrine of sin is outmoded?"

The young man said, "No."

Dr. Leavell said, "Don't you think you had better get down on your knees and ask God to forgive you of sin and to ask the Lord Jesus Christ to come into your heart?"

The young man confessed his sin. He asked the Lord Jesus Christ to come into his heart, and when he did, the grace of God functioned as it always will in the individual who opens his heart to Christ. The young man became a new creation in Christ Jesus, and when he stood up he said, "Dr. Leavell, if you hadn't made a fool out of me, I never would have believed." That young man became a fine husband and father, a lay leader in his church, and a noted evangelical lay-Christian. Why? Because he let the grace of God function in his life.[1]

---

1 Cited by Harold L. Fickett, Jr., "The Grace of God," *Founder's Week Conference Messages* (Chicago: Moody Bible Institute, 1958) 180–182.

THE HEART IS . . . DESPERATELY WICKED

Some console themselves that they have never committed murder or theft. This may be technically true, but what they *are* is much worse than what they *have done*. There is no sin of which they are not capable. There is an evil, corrupt nature within that is deceitful and desperately wicked above all things (Jeremiah 17:9).

Furthermore, from God's standpoint we are not just sinners—we are desperately wicked. We are depraved in every area of our lives—in thought, word, and deed. We are guilty of breaking all of God's commandments.

The law is like a chain of ten links. When one link is broken, the whole chain is broken.

> For whoever shall keep the whole law, and yet stumble in one point, he is guilty of all (James 2:10 NKJV).

It is useless to talk about a spark of goodness in every man. God sees none (see Romans 3:12).

Instead, he describes us as being ungodly, deceitful, wicked, enemies, lost, evildoers, guilty, unthankful, vile, covetous, and abominable. He catalogs a few of the sins of men as uncleanness, irreverence, immorality, idolatry, witchcraft, hatred, wrath, strife, seditions, heresies, envyings, murders, drunkenness, revelings, unbelief, and lying (see Galatians 5:19–21).

Nowhere in all literature is the sinful nature of man more graphically and faithfully laid bare than in Romans 3:10–20.

Man's true character was also revealed at Calvary when creatures nailed their Creator to a criminal's cross and watched him dying there (Matthew 27:35–36). The death of the Son of God was the natural sequel to their rejection of him as rightful ruler.

MAN IS HELPLESS . . . APART FROM GOD

Not only is man sunk in ruin, misery, and shame, but he is utterly unable to do anything about it. He is ungodly, but he is also without strength (Romans 5:6).

Therefore, if man is left to his own devices, he will perish eternally as a sinner (Psalm 9:17). If he gets what he deserves, it will be hell forever.

In other words, God must intervene if man is to be saved from endless damnation. And this is exactly why God has provided the spiritual miracle known as the new birth.

A dying obstetrician called for his minister. He was deeply troubled because he knew he was not ready to meet God. When the minister came the doctor said, "I am dying. I know it. I've heard somewhere about being born again. Can you tell me something about it?"

The minister was somewhat liberal in his theology and he said, "It's true the Bible does speak about being born again, but that is not for men like you. You've lived a wonderful life in the community, and there is no reason for you to fear."

He said, "Oh, deep down in my heart I feel a sense of guilt and condemnation before God, and something must be done."

"But, sir, you've done good works; you've been a leader in the community."

"I know, but what about this being born again? I somehow have the feeling that that might be a help for me."

"But you are a good religious man."

Finally the doctor looked at him and said, "You know, I've brought many children into this world, and many a time I've looked at a baby and said, 'That child has a future, but it has no past.' The Bible speaks about being born again, and somehow I feel that if I could possibly lay hold of this new birth I could have a future and no past, and that's what I need."

3

The Problem

Can God Be both Just and Merciful?

In considering the subject of salvation, we face a very real problem at this point: How can a holy God save guilty sinners and still be just in doing so?

Consider once again who God is! He is the holy, righteous sovereign of the universe (1 Peter 1: 16), who can do only what is honest, fair, equitable, and proper (Genesis 18:25).

Dr. Tozer says of the holiness of God:

> Holy is the way God is. To be holy He does not conform to a standard. He is absolutely holy with an infinite, incomprehensible fullness of purity that is incapable of being other than it is. Because He is holy,

27

all His attributes are holy; that is, whatever we think of as belonging to God must be thought of as holy. God is holy and has made holiness the moral condition necessary to the health of His universe. [1]

Think what it means for God to be holy. Job 15:15 says of God that even "the heavens are not clean in his sight." And Isaiah reminds us that the shining seraphim hide their faces in their wings when confronted with the uncreated fire of God's holiness (Isaiah 6:2–3).

Then consider who and what man is! He is a poor, wretched, miserable sinner, cut off from God, dead in trespasses and in sins, and bound for everlasting ruin (Matthew 25:41, 46). No wonder Isaiah said: "Woe is me, for I am undone! Because I am a man of unclean lips," when he *came* to realize how holy God is (Isaiah 6:5).

Most people feel uncomfortable in the presence of a truly good man. How terrible it must be to be brought into the presence of a holy God.

GOD'S STANDARD IS ABSOLUTE PERFECTION

Because God is righteous and holy, he can allow only sinless people to dwell with him in heaven (Ephesians 5:5). His standard is absolute perfection, and he can permit only perfect people to fellowship with him (Hebrews 12:14). Ungodly people cannot approach him (Revelation 21:27). He is "of purer eyes than to behold evil, and cannot look on wickedness" (Habakkuk 1:13 NKJV).

---

1 A. W. Tozer, *The Knowledge of the Holy* (New York: Harper & Brothers, 1961), 113.

This standard is reflected in the Ten Commandments (Exodus 20:1–17) and in the Sermon on the Mount (Matthew 5–7), which passages you should carefully read at this point. People who imagine they can live up to the standard of absolute moral and spiritual perfection embodied in these utterances are self-deceived.

MAN CANNOT MEET GOD'S STANDARD

Saul of Tarsus (later the famous apostle Paul) thought he could meet the standard, but later he wrote:

> I had not known sin, but by the law; for I had not known covetousness unless the law had said, "You shall not covet (Romans 7:7 NKJV).

He measured himself alongside God's standard and realized he had come short.

Man simply cannot achieve perfection or sinlessness by his own efforts.

> Who can say, "I have made my heart clean, I am pure from my sin"? (Proverbs 20:9).

Nothing that he can ever do will win him favor with God.

> For though you wash yourself with lye and use much soap, yet your iniquity is marked before Me, says the Lord GOD (Jeremiah 2:22 NKJV).

Neither by good works nor by tears and prayers can his sins be erased.

GOD MUST PUNISH SIN

Can he approve man's sin? Certainly not!

> The way of the wicked is an abomination unto the
> Lord (Proverbs 15:9).

He would not be God if he allowed evil. If a judge condones a criminal act, he condemns himself.

Can God overlook man's sin? Emphatically no! To do so would violate his holy character. He marks sin every time it is committed (Job 10:14; Revelation 18:5; Jeremiah 2:22).

Can he excuse sin? There is only one answer. His throne would no longer be holy if he passed over that which is evil (Genesis 18:23–25; Isaiah 6:1–7).

Can he forgive sin where no penalty has been paid? No! He must act righteously; to forgive sin without adequate satisfaction would be, in itself, a sinful act, and God cannot sin (1 John 1:5). It has been truly said that if God forgave sin without an atonement justice would be sacrificed and abandoned; the law would cease to have any terrors for the guilty; and its penalty would be purposeless.

There is only one attitude that the Lord can take toward sin. He must punish it (Isaiah 13:11). He can "not at all acquit the wicked" (Nahum 1:3). When his holy law is broken, the offender must be punished; the claims of the law must be fully satisfied.

Sin is a serious matter. In his great penitential prayer, David said to God:

> I acknowledged my sin to you, and my iniquity I have
> not hid. I said, "I will confess my transgressions unto
> the Lord," and You forgave the iniquity of my sin"
> (Psalm 32:5 NKJV).

Note how often he comes back to the subject of his sin.

There are three Hebrew words used in this verse to depict sin and they illustrate its various aspects.

Sin denotes "missing the mark." It underlines man's general condition of unfitness for God's presence.

Transgression is a stronger word and has in it the thought of open rebellion against God. The word for *iniquity* comes out of a root word signifying "crooked" and underlines the "bentness" of human character. The word *depravity* perhaps best embodies its meaning. Thus *failure, revolt* and *natural bias* are all involved in the Psalmist's indictment of himself. No wonder God must punish sin.

The penalty for breaking the law of God is death. "The soul who sins shall die" (Ezekiel 18:4, 20 NKJV). "The wages of sin is death" (Romans 6:23). There is no escape from this sentence. God has said it in the first place, and he must see that the sentence is carried out. He must be faithful to his own Word.

GOD LOVES THE SINNER

Yet the Lord is a God of love (1 John 4:8). We must never forget this. He is "not willing that any should perish, but that all should come to repentance" (2 Peter 3:9). He longs to show mercy to the sinner (Ephesians 2:4). How can he do it?

THE PROBLEM SUMMARIZED

This, then, is the problem. A *holy* God says, "The sinner must be punished by death." But the same God is a *loving* God, and he says: "I want to show mercy to the sinner. I want to save him. I want to regard the ill-deserving as if he were innocent. I want to have him with me in heaven for eternity." God is holy; he hates sin. But God is love; he loves the sinner. How can he save the sinner and still act in a righteous, holy way?

1. *God's holiness and righteousness demand that*

    a. *Only sinless, perfect people be admitted to heaven.*

    b. *Sinners be punished by death.*

2. *God's love, mercy, and grace prompt him to*

    a. *Save the sinner from his deserved doom.*

    b. *Make him fit for a home in heaven.*

WHAT IS THE LORD GOING TO DO?

One fact is certain! If God allows the sinner to pay the price of his sins, he will perish forever and be cut off from the presence of God.

In Scotland it used to be the custom at harvest time for women to help in binding the sheaves. A woman named Hannah Lamond offered her services; and since she had no one to tend her baby, she brought her child along and found for him a cozy little crib in a corner of the field. An eagle spotted the unattended child and, swooping down, seized the child in its talons and carried it to its nest high on a rocky cliff. The bird was seen and the alarm given, but nobody could climb the heights to the eagle's nest. Several men tried, including a sailor who was used to climbing heights. At last the mother determined to try. Impelled by her mother love, she edged her way upward until she reached the nest. Then, fearless in defense of her babe, she fought off the eagle and snatched her little one, still unharmed, from the nest. Slowly and with infinite patience and perseverance she groped her way back to the ground to be received with rejoicing by her friends. Love found a way. When all other helpers failed, love found a way.

Now God loves the sinner far more than Hannah Lamond loved her baby. The God who planted creature love in a mother's heart can surely find a way to bring back to himself the lost sons of Adam's fallen race.

4

The Solution— Substitution

Is a Just Solution Possible?

Man's situation seems to be hopeless. He cannot atone for his own sins. Yet, if he suffers the consequences, he will be doomed and damned forever.

But God is gracious. He has no pleasure in the death of the wicked (Ezekiel 33:11). Judgment is his strange work (Isaiah 28:11). He must devise a way in which man can be spared, that "His banished ones are not expelled from Him" (2 Samuel 14:14 NKJV).

Is it possible that a just solution can be found to the

problem? Can the great God of the universe satisfy his love without sacrificing his holiness? Yes, it is conceivable, for instance, that a *substitute* could die for a person, and by thus paying the penalty of his sins, permit the guilty one to go free.

The principle has often been illustrated in times of war. During the Napoleonic wars, a Frenchman was drafted and sent to a place to which he did not want to go. A friend volunteered to take his place, enlisted in the draftee's name, was sent to the battle zone, and died in action.

Some time later Napoleon wanted more men, and, by some mistake, the first man was drafted a second time. The man claimed he could not go because he was dead! A search was made of the records and, sure enough, the man was listed as dead and buried. The law had no more claim upon him. A substitute had died in his place.

A BIBLICAL ILLUSTRATION OF SUBSTITUTION

The idea of substitution is also strikingly illustrated in a well-known passage of the Old Testament. It is the account of the testing of Abraham's faith by the offering up of his only son, Isaac, to God (Genesis 22:1–14). Here is how the account ends.

> Then they came to the place of which God had told him. And Abraham built an altar there and placed the wood in order; and he bound Isaac his son and laid him on the altar, upon the wood. And Abraham stretched out his hand and took the knife to slay his son. But the Angel of the Lord called to him from heaven and said, "Abraham, Abraham!" So he said, "Here I am." And He said, "Do not lay your hand on

the lad, or do anything to him; for now I know that you fear God, since you have not withheld your son, your only son, from Me." Then Abraham lifted his eyes and looked, and there behind him was a ram caught in a thicket by its horns. So Abraham went and took the ram, and offered it up for a burnt offering instead of his son. And Abraham called the name of the place, The-Lord-Will-Provide; as it is said to this day, "In the Mount of The Lord it shall be provided" (Genesis 22:9–14 NKJV).

Here you have substitution. "Abraham went and took the ram, and offered him up for a burnt-offering in the stead of his son" (v. 13). However, this is only a type of the substitute needed by man. The picture is imperfect in the sense that a ram's death would not suffice for a man. But it is valuable in the sense that it shows how substitution works.

Now if substitution is to be used in the plan of man's salvation, the question naturally arises, "Who is to be the substitute? Who is qualified to take man's place?"

MAN'S SUBSTITUTE MUST BE A MAN

Actually, the field of possibilities is very limited. Could an angel die for man? A moment of consideration will convince us that this would not be possible. For one thing, as far as we know, angels, being spirits, cannot die. Whoever is man's substitute must become "lower than the angels for the suffering of death" (Hebrews 2:9). Then, even if an angel could die, man's worship would be directed to a creature, and this is forbidden by the Word of God (Exodus 20:5).

Well, then, could not an animal die for man? In the Old Testament animal sacrifices were commanded, but it must be remembered that they were *not sufficient* to put away a single sin. "It is not possible that the blood of bulls and of goats should take away sins" (Hebrews 10:4). Animal sacrifices were simply *pictures* or *types* of the perfect sacrifice who was to come.

Neither angels nor animals can take the place of man in bearing the punishment of his sins. Since the substitute must be of the same kind, it remains that man must die for man. This is absolutely essential. Any other arrangement would be unequal, unfair, unjust.

He must be sinless

But now there is another problem. One sinful man cannot die for another, because he must be punished for his own iniquities. God's law demands the death of every transgressor. The only satisfactory substitute must therefore be a sinless man.

He must be infinite— and only God is infinite

And even then, we must add another qualification. One sinless man could righteously take the place of *only one* sinner. The substitute needed by the human race must die for all mankind. His death must, therefore, have infinite power and value. By that we mean that it must be sufficient in its merit to take care of all the sins that ever have been and ever will be committed. The substitute must be infinite, and this brings us to the obvious truth that only God is infinite.

HE MUST SHED HIS BLOOD

One final requirement. If man's sins are to be blotted out of God's sight, the substitute must shed his blood. That this is a requirement of God's character and ways is proved by the following verses of Scripture:

> Now the blood shall be a sign for you on the houses where you are. And when I see the blood, I will pass over you; and the plague shall not be on you to destroy you when I strike the land of Egypt (Exodus 12:13 NKJV).

> For the life of the flesh is in the blood, and I have given it to you upon the altar to make atonement for your souls; for it is the blood that makes atonement for the soul (Leviticus 17:11 NKJV).

> And according to the law almost all things are purified with blood, and without shedding of blood there is no remission (Hebrews 9:22 NKJV).

TO SUMMARIZE

1. It is conceivable that God could save sinners if a substitute died in their place.

2. Such a substitute must meet certain stringent requirements: (a) He would not be an angel or an animal. This would be an unequal exchange. (b) He must therefore be a man. (c) However, he must be a sinless man; else he must die for his own sins. (d) He must be infinite if he is to die for an innumerable company of sinners. Because only God is infinite, he must be both God and man. (e) He must be willing to take the sinner's place and bear his

punishment. (f) In doing this, he must shed his blood, because sins cannot be remitted in any other way.

THE LORD JESUS IS SUCH A SUBSTITUTE

Now the glorious news of the Gospel is that just such a substitute has been provided. The Lord Jesus Christ is his name. Notice how wonderfully he meets the need of sinners.

1. Is he man? Yes, for he took "the form of a servant," and came "in the likeness of men" (Philippians 2:7). God sent "His own Son in the likeness of sinful flesh" (Romans 8:3). "The Word became flesh, and dwelt among us" (John 1:14 NKJV).

2. Is he sinless? Yes, he "was in all points tempted as we are, yet without sin" (Hebrews 4:15; see also John 8:46).

5

The Finished Work

The substitutionary death of the Lord Jesus Christ on Golgotha—together with His glorious resurrection—is the most important and most significant event of all history. It is the dividing point upon which two eras converge— one which looked forward to it and the other which gazes back upon it.

CHRIST FORETOLD AS THE SINNER'S SUBSTITUTE

Throughout the Old Testament Scriptures, the substitutionary death of Christ was anticipated by types and shadows and also by direct prophetic statements. Perhaps none of the Old Testament writers described the person and work of Christ more clearly than Isaiah. Certainly none predicted more fully that he would die for the sins of others than this faithful preacher. In the fifty-third chapter of his prophecy, the truth of substitution is taught at least eleven times. Verses four through eight, particularly, abound in references to it.

> Surely He has borne our griefs
> And carried our sorrows;
> Yet we esteemed Him stricken,
> Smitten by God, and afflicted.
> But He was wounded for our transgressions,
> He was bruised for our iniquities;
> The chastisement for our peace was upon Him,
> And by His stripes we are healed.
> All we like sheep have gone astray;
> We have turned, every one, to his own way;
> And the LORD has laid on Him the iniquity of us all.
> He was oppressed and He was afflicted,
> Yet He opened not His mouth;
> He was led as a lamb to the slaughter,
> And as a sheep before its shearers is silent,
> So He opened not His mouth.
> He was taken from prison and from judgment,
> And who will declare His generation?
> For He was cut off from the land of the living;
> For the transgressions of My people He was stricken
> (Isaiah 53:4–8 NKJV).

CHRIST REVEALED AS THE SINNER'S SUBSTITUTE

Then, turning to the New Testament, we find this great doctrine repeated over and over again. Three important passages will show the emphasis that God places upon it.

1. In 2 Corinthians 8:9 (NKJV) we read:

For you know the grace of our Lord Jesus Christ, that though He was rich, yet *for your sakes* He became poor, that you through His poverty might become rich.

Christ was rich in the past eternity, dwelling in uninterrupted bliss in heaven (Proverbs 8:22–31). He became poor when he entered this world as a babe; when he lived so humbly that he did not have a place of his own on which to lay his head (Matthew 8:20); and, above all, when he died in loneliness and shame on Calvary. He did all this for us, that we might be blessed with the riches of eternal life and a home in heaven.

2. We are told again in 2 Corinthians 5:21 (NKJV):

For He [God] made Him [Christ] who knew no sin to be sin for us, that we might become the righteousness of God in Him.

In a way that we cannot understand, God caused our sins to be placed on the Lord Jesus Christ. The Savior did not, of course, become sinful, but he bore the guilt and penalty of our sins. Our sins were not *in* him, but they were on him.

He suffered God's judgment for those sins, so that God might have a just way of making us righteous in Christ.

3. The apostle Peter emphasizes this same truth:

For Christ also suffered once for sins, *the just for the unjust,* that He might bring us to God, being put to death in the flesh but made alive by the Spirit (1 Peter 3:18 NKJV).

Here the Savior is spoken of as suffering for sins; but lest anyone should think it was for his own sins, the apostle quickly adds, "the just for the unjust." He suffered in the place of others to provide a righteous way to bring them to God. In doing this, he was put to death as far as his body was concerned, but raised from the dead by the Holy Spirit.

A FINISHED REDEMPTION

In connection with the sacrifice of the Lord Jesus on the cross, it is of extreme importance to realize that he not only died in the place of sinners but that he also completely finished the work necessary for their salvation.

Many passages of Scripture announce this glorious fact. For instance:

> I have glorified You on the earth. I have finished the work which You have given Me to do (John 17:4 NKJV).

> So when Jesus had received the sour wine, He said, 'It is finished!' and bowing His head He gave up His spirit (John 19:30 NKJV).

> But this Man, after He had offered one sacrifice for sins forever, sat down on the right hand of God (Hebrews 10:12 NKJV).

Think for a moment of all that was accomplished by his work on Calvary!

1. The full demands of the law were met (Romans 3:31). The law demanded absolute obedience or the punishment of death. Sinners had all failed to keep the law; therefore, they deserved death. The Savior bore the penalty that they deserved. Therefore, when they accept the Savior, the law can demand no more. They are "dead" to the law (Romans 7:4).

2. God's righteousness and holiness were satisfied (Psalm 85:10). Sin has been punished. A way has been found whereby sinners can be freed from their sins, and thus made fit for the presence of God.

3. The redeeming work of Christ was sufficient to save all the sinners of all time (1 John 2:2). This does not mean that all will be saved. Only those who trust him are converted (1 John 5:12). But his work is of such infinite value and power that, if all sinners did believe on him, he could save them all (Hebrews 7:5).

4. Finally, God's love can go out to sinners without violating his holiness. He has found a just and equitable way of saving sinners (Romans 3:6).

THE SINNER'S RESPONSIBILITY: ACCEPTANCE OF GOD'S GIFT BY FAITH

Since Christ has so marvelously finished the work of redemption, the sinner need not add to it. All that is necessary to take a soul to heaven has been accomplished. Our responsibility is to accept what has been done, to receive the gift of God by faith.

We cannot add to a finished work. We have previously seen that an unsaved person *cannot* do anything to win eternal life from God. Here the joyous truth is that *he does not have to* do a thing.

A Christian had been urging a carpenter friend of his to accept Christ as personal Savior. The carpenter had resisted all the Christian's appeals, arguing that he had to *do* something for salvation, not just accept it as a gift. The Christian explained that the work of salvation was complete and needed only to be accepted, but still the craftsman could not see it. The conversation was taking place in the carpenter's shop. Seeing that his friend had just completed a magnificent mahogany table, the Christian decided to illustrate his point in a forceful way. He picked up a saw and hammer and walked over to the table, shining in its latest coat of wax. He acted as if he were about to mar the table with the tools. The craftsman was horrified. "Don't touch it," he cried, "You'll spoil it. It's finished!"

"Yes, my friend," said the Christian, "and that's exactly how it is with the work of Christ. It's finished. If you touch it, you spoil it. You cannot add to a finished work." The craftsman saw the point at once, and immediately received Christ.

> *I am not told to labor*
> *To put away my sin;*
> *So foolish, weak and helpless,*
> *I never could begin.*
> *But blessed truth—I know it!*
> *Though ruined by the Fall,*
> *Christ for my soul hath suffered;*
> *Yes, Christ has done it all.*

IS GOD SATISFIED? WITNESS THE RESURRECTION OF CHRIST!

One final question remains. Is God satisfied with the finished work of his beloved Son? He has given us unmistakable proof that he is completely satisfied, by the fact that he raised Christ from the dead (1 Corinthians 15:3–8, 12–22).

46

IS THE BELIEVER JUSTIFIED? WITNESS THE RESURRECTION OF CHRIST!

The resurrection is our guarantee. "Jesus our Lord . . . was delivered up for our offenses, and was raised again for our justification" (Romans 4:24–25).

If the Lord had remained in the tomb, we should have no hope beyond the grave. "If Christ is not raised, your faith is futile—you are still in your sins" (1 Corinthians 15:17 NKJV). There is no salvation in a dead Messiah. But God raised Christ from the dead as proof that his work was accepted, and that all who trust him will follow him in resurrection.

CALVARY—LOVE'S PROVISION FOR THE DEMANDS OF A HOLY GOD

Is it not true that God has spanned a mighty gulf at Calvary? His love provided what his righteousness demanded. The sinner appropriates salvation by faith. God counts him righteous, and a state of peace then exists between the two. As Albert Midlane considered God's "easy, artless, unencumbered plan" of salvation, he summarized it beautifully in the following stanzas:

> *The perfect righteousness of God*
> *Is witnessed in the Saviour's blood;*
> *'Tis in the cross of Christ we trace*
> *His righteousness, yet wondrous grace.*
>
> *God could not pass the sinner by;*
> *His sin demands that he must die;*

But in the cross of Christ we see
How God can save, yet righteous be.

The sin alights on Jesus' head;
'Tis in His blood sin's debt is paid;
Stern Justice can demand no more,
And Mercy can dispense her store.

The sinner who believes is free,
Can say, "The Saviour died for me";
Can point to the atoning blood,
And say, "This made my peace with God."

6

Amazing Grace

What Is Grace?

Webster defines "grace" as "favor," "kindness," or "mercy." Theologians define it as "unmerited favor." Under grace God does not treat us as we deserve but according to his lovingkindness.

During the days of the revolutionary war, there lived in Ephrata, Pennsylvania, a preacher named Peter Miller. He was a personal friend of George Washington. There also lived in this town a man named Michael Wittman who detested the preacher and did everything he could do to defame and oppose him. It so happened that Wittman became involved in treason, was arrested, and sentenced to death. When Miller heard of it he walked the entire seventy miles to Philadelphia to plead with Washington for Wittman's life. "Peter," said George Washington, "I cannot grant you the life of your friend." Miller explained that Wittman was not his friend but his bitterest foe.

On hearing this Washington, deeply moved, agreed to pardon the delinquent. Wittman was released and went back to Ephrata with Miller, no longer his foe but his friend.

This is grace! This is how God treats sinners today. As we have seen, God's holiness has been satisfied by the death of his Son on our behalf. Now he can extend to us his grace.

WHY SUCH LOVE?

But why did God send his only begotten Son to die for guilty man? Why did the Lord Jesus consent to give his life a ransom for many? Why was Heaven's best given for earth's worst? Why did such a worthy person serve as the substitute for such unworthy sinners?

IT WAS UNMERITED

Was it because man deserved it? Assuredly not. God's gift of love was entirely unmerited, as far as sinners are concerned. The creature has no claim on God whatever. In fact, there is positive demerit on man's side. Man has broken God's law and is therefore an enemy of God. There would have been ample cause if God had condemned him forever. Certainly there was no worthiness about man that called for the sacrifice at Calvary.

GOD DID NOT NEED MAN

Was it because God needed man? Ridiculous. God is utterly independent and self-contained; he does not need anyone or anything. Did God need our services? He could have made machines that would never have disappointed him. Did he need our personalities, our good looks, our talents? If so, he could create millions more like us who would serve him more acceptably. Did he need our money? He answers:

> Every beast of the forest is Mine, And the cattle on a thousand hills. . . . If I were hungry, I would not tell you: for the world is Mine, and all its fullness (Psalm 50:10, 12 NKJV).

God brought worlds into being without man's help (Isaiah 40:13–14; Job 38:4), and does he now need the help of this frail creature of dust?

MAN DID NOT SEEK GOD

Did God love us because we sought him? On the contrary, we said in our hearts,

> Depart from us,
> For we do not desire the knowledge of Your ways
> (Job 21:14 NKJV).

Paul affirms this attitude:

> There is none who seeks after God (Romans 3:11 NKJV).

When he sent his messengers to us with the gospel, we

rejected them openly. When he sent his Son, we cast him out of the city and crucified him, crying:

> We will not have this man to reign over us (Luke 19:14).

> In this is love, not that we loved God, but that He loved us and sent His Son to be the propitiation for our sins (1 John 4:10 NKJV).

GOD SOUGHT NO REWARD

Well, then, did the Lord show mercy to us because he hoped for something in return? Again we must answer, "No." God's purposes in redemption were entirely unselfish. He knew we had nothing to pay (Luke 7:42). He knew he could never be rewarded for such an amazing gift.

GOD WAS INDEBTED TO NONE

But was not God somehow indebted to man? Indeed he was not. He is indebted to no one.

> Who has first given to Him
> And it shall be repaid to him?
> For of Him and through Him and to Him are all things,
> to whom be glory forever
> (Romans 11:35–36 NKJV).

Let us face the fact that God knew we were morally and spiritually bankrupt. He knew that we never would be converted if he did not provide salvation as a free, unconditional, and outright gift.

He did not have to do it. As Spurgeon so aptly expressed it:

What is it to the infinite Jehovah whether thou serve Him or not? If thou rebel against God, will He be less glorious? If thou wilt not obey the Lord, what difference can it make to His boundless happiness? Will His crown shine the less brightly, or His heaven be less resplendent because thou choosest to be a rebel against Him? . . . If a gnat should contend with yonder blast furnace, you know what the end would be. It is for thine own sake that God would have thee yield to Him; how can it be for His own?

WHY SUCH GRACE?

Why then did he do it? There is only one answer. It was grace unspeakable; love unbounded; mercy, vast, full, and free (Romans 5:8). There can be no other explanation of why the perfect joy, bliss, and fellowship of heaven were interrupted when the Lord Jesus came into the world as a spotless Man and died in agony and shame on Calvary's cruel cross to redeem us to God. Amazing grace—that is what it was. It was God's choosing to save us simply because he wanted to. It was God's loving us simply because he chose to do so (John 3:16).

UNFATHOMABLE GRACE!

None of us can understand it. All we can do at present is stand in awe and wonder at the mystery of Golgotha— and worship. Throughout eternity God will show us more clearly "the exceeding riches of his grace in his kindness toward us through Christ Jesus" (Ephesians 2:7).

As a sailor, John Newton lived and worked with as wild and rough a crew as ever went to sea. He himself lived a wicked life, sinking lower and lower, despite the prayers of his loved ones at home, until at last he became the slave of a slave—in the power of a native African woman who delighted to make him beg for his very bread. After his conversion, Newton became a preacher and a renowned hymn writer. One of his most famous hymns looks back to the days when God's grace found him in all his sin and need and looks forward to the eternity of bliss that divine grace made possible for his soul:

> *Amazing grace! how sweet the sound,*
> *That saved a wretch like me!*
> *I once was lost, but now am found,*
> *Was blind, but now I see.*
>
> *'Twas grace that taught my heart to fear,*
> *And grace my fears relieved;*
> *How precious did that grace appear*
> *The hour I first believed.*
>
> *Through many dangers, toils and, snares,*
> *I have already come;*
> *'Tis grace hath brought me safe thus far,*
> *And grace will lead me home.*
>
> *When we've been there ten thousand years,*
> *Bright shining as the sun,*
> *We've no less days to sing God's praise*
> *Than when we'd first begun.*

7

The Way of Salvation

A Free Gift—Received by Faith

We have seen how Christ has done all that is necessary to provide redemption for sinners. God's salvation is offered by him as a free gift (Romans 6:3). The sinner's responsibility is to accept what has been done. God would not populate heaven with unwilling men. In that case, it would not be heaven. They would be as miserable as hardened sinners in a prayer meeting.

The method chosen by God for receiving eternal life is simple faith (Romans 5:1). It is not by good works, not by good character, not by church membership or anything of man's endeavor, but simply and only by believing on the Lord Jesus Christ (Ephesians 2:8–9). Everyone can be saved in this way, and no one can be saved in any other way (John 14:6; Hebrews 11:6).

FAITH COMES BY HEARING THE WORD OF GOD

First of all, there must be the Word of God (2 Timothy 3:15). No one can be converted apart from the Bible. It may be as the Scriptures are preached from a pulpit, quoted by a relative or friend, or read in a tract or book. However, the gospel story must be known, and it can be known only as revealed in the Bible. Not only must the gospel be heard, but it must be received as the very Word of God (1 Thessalonians 2:13). As the Scriptures are read, God gives the faith to receive them. Thus "faith [comes] by hearing, and hearing by the word of God" (Romans 10:17).

When a person reads the Bible, he may discover several statements that he does not like. First, he learns that he is a sinner (Isaiah 64:6). That is distasteful to him. Next he learns that he cannot save himself (Romans 9:16). This hurts his pride. Finally, he is told that only the Lord Jesus can save him (Isaiah 45:21–22). But he does not want to submit to the Son of God (John 5:40). Thus, if left to himself, man would never accept the gospel.

THE HOLY SPIRIT USES THE WORD OF GOD TO CONVICT THE SINNER

But here something unique happens. The Holy Spirit

uses the Word of God in some way, mysterious to us, to produce conviction in the heart of the sinner (John 16:7–11). He convicts man of the truth of the Scriptures, of his lost and hopeless condition, of the peril of dying without Christ. This is generally known as conviction of sin. In some cases, it is marked by deep anguish of soul; in others only by a simple realization that one is lost and needs to be saved.

The sinner is thereby brought to an end of himself (Luke 15:17–21). He despairs of salvation by self-effort. He sees no hope in himself (Luke 18:13). In fact, he takes sides with God against himself and acknowledges that he is indeed a sinner and therefore worthy of everlasting punishment (Psalm 51:1–5).

John Bunyan knew this all too well from personal experience. He begins his immortal classic, *Pilgrim's Progress*, by underlining the fact that conviction of sin comes from reading the Word of God. He said:

> I dreamed, and behold, I saw a man clothed with rags, standing in a certain place . . . a book in his hand, and a great burden upon his back. I looked and saw him open the book, and not being able longer to contain, he brake out with a lamentable cry, saying, "What shall I do?"[1]

Bunyan then describes the effect that the pilgrim's conviction had, not only on himself but on others. He tells us that the more Christian read, the greater his burden became. At last, he met a man called Evangelist to whom he unburdened his fears. "Sir," he said to Evangel-

---

1 John Bunyan, *Pilgrim's Progress*, (Philadelphia: Charles Foster Publishing Company, 1891), 53–54.

ist, "I perceive by the book in my hand, that I am condemned to die, and after that to come to judgment; and I find that I am not willing to do the first, nor able to do the second."[2]

THE HOLY SPIRIT USES THE WORD OF GOD TO TELL OF CHRIST

But the Holy Spirit never leaves a soul in that condition. He next shows him that the Lord Jesus Christ is the very Savior he needs (John 1:29) and invites him to receive the Son of God as Lord and Savior by faith (Revelation 22:17).

What do we mean by saving faith? Saving faith is simply trust in the Lord Jesus. It is, as someone has said, "affectionate confidence." When a drowning man clings to a log, he puts all his hope in that log. The letters of the word itself have been used to explain what faith is—Forsaking All I Take Him. When a man sits in a chair, he rests on the finished work of the carpenter. When he boards an airplane, he rests his whole weight on it. Previously he might have believed all about the value and power of the plane, but he does not really trust it until he boards it for flight.

In *Pilgrim's Progress,* Christian came at last to the place where his sins could be removed. He came to Calvary. Bunyan described it thus:

> Now, I saw in my dream that the highway up which Christian was to go was fenced on either side with a wall that was called Salvation. Up this way, therefore

---

2 *Ibid.,* 56

did burdened Christian run, but not without great difficulty, because of the load on his back.

He ran thus till he came to a place somewhat ascending; and upon that place stood a cross, and a little below, in the bottom, a sepulchre. So I saw in my dream, that just as Christian came up with the cross, his burden loosed from off his shoulders, and fell from off his back, and began to tumble, and so continued to do till it came to the mouth of the Sepulchre, where it fell in, and I saw it no more."[3] Bunyan tells us how the pilgrim, loosed of the heavy burden of his sin forever, went on his way rejoicing. And as he went, he sang:

> *Thus far did I come laden with my sin;*
> *Nor could aught ease the grief that I was in,*
> *Till I came hither: what a place is this!*
> *Must here be the beginning of my bliss?*
> *Must here the burden fall from off my back:*
> *Must here the strings that bound it to me crack?*
> *Blest cross! blest sepulchre! blest rather be*
> *The Man that there was put to shame for me!*[4]

SALVATION—A DIVINE FACT

The first time a person ever acknowledges that he is a sinner and believes on the Lord Jesus Christ, he is saved; he is born again; he is converted (Romans 10:9). The marvelous transaction takes place sometimes without any

---

3 *Ibid.,* 91.
4 *Ibid.,* 92.

outward show. He may not feel any different because salvation is not simply a matter of feelings; it is a divine fact. The infallible Word of God says that all who trust the Savior receive eternal life; that they shall never come into condemnation but have passed from death unto life (John 5:24).

THE LORD JESUS—THE OBJECT OF FAITH

It is not the amount of a person's faith that matters. Some have great faith; others only a spark. It is not faith that saves, but the object of faith, namely, the Lord Jesus. Whenever God sees a person with the merest speck of faith in his Son, he gives eternal life.

WE ARE THE SINNERS; CHRIST IS THE SAVIOR

There is absolutely nothing a sinner can do to merit salvation (Ephesians 2:8–9). The idea that he can somehow do or be something to please God is natural to man. But when a person comes to Christ for salvation, he brings nothing but sin and guilt. It has been well said, "We do all the sinning; Christ does all the saving." If a sinner insists on standing before God on the ground of his own fitness, he will get what he deserves (Revelation 20:12).

The true attitude of a contrite, repentant sinner coming to Christ for salvation is nobly expressed in the words of a well-known hymn. Thousands have trusted the Redeemer with these words in their hearts and on their lips.

> *Just as I am, without one plea*
> *But that Thy blood was shed for me,*

And that Thou bid'st me come to Thee—
O Lamb of God, I come, I come!

Just as I am—poor, wretched, blind!
Sight, riches, healing of the mind,
Yea, all I need in Thee to find,
O Lamb of God, I come, I come!

Just as I am, Thou wilt receive,
Wilt welcome, pardon, cleanse, relieve!
Because Thy promise I believe—
O Lamb of God, I come, I come!

Just as I am—Thy love unknown
Has broken every barrier down;
Now to be Thine, yea, Thine alone,
O Lamb of God, I come, I come!

—Charlotte Elliott

8

The Rock Beneath

An elderly Christian woman was dying. For many years she had been trusting the Lord Jesus for salvation and resting all her hopes on him. He was the Rock of her salvation (Psalm 62:2, 6). Now, in her last moments, her friends gathered around her bed.

"She's sinking fast," said one.

The woman heard the remark and whispered in reply, "You cannot sink through Rock!"

The question we now face is whether salvation is forever, or whether a person can be saved and then lost again.

There are those who maintain that when a person is genuinely saved, he is saved forever.

Others believe that this is a very dangerous doctrine that will lead Christians into lives of sin. They state that one's salvation depends on one's life and that to sin would be to forfeit eternal life.

If a person truly understands the gospel of the grace of God, he will readily see that the first view is the correct one. Anyone who is genuinely saved is saved forever.

The following Scriptural truths teach that the believer is eternally secure.

GREAT FACTS

1. Salvation depends not on what we do for God but on what he has done for us. It depends on the finished work of the Lord Jesus on the Cross. That was a perfect and complete work (Hebrews 10:12). It cannot be added to or improved upon (Hebrews 10:18). To doubt eternal security is to dishonor the sufficiency of the Lord's atoning work.

The believer's acceptance is in Christ, not in himself. Therefore, it is a perfect and complete acceptance (Hebrews 10:14). It is as eternal as Christ himself.

The truth of acceptance is illustrated in the world of nature. A shepherd may have a sheep whose lamb has died. At the same time he may also have a lamb whose mother has died. This poses a problem for the shepherd. How can he raise the orphan lamb? The obvious solution would be to give it to the sheep that has lost her lamb. But this won't work; the sheep will not accept the lamb or feed it because she knows it is not her own. So the Shepherd takes the skin of the dead lamb and ties it around the living lamb, then gently nudges it over to the sheep. She bends over, sniffs the lamb, and eventually accepts it. But why? Isn't it the same lamb she had previously rejected? Yes, but now the lamb has come to her clothed in her own lamb. She accepts it not because of what it is in itself, but because it is *in her lamb.*

The parallel is obvious. God accepts the believing sinner not because of what he is, but because he comes clothed in all the merits and virtues of the Lamb of God who bears away the sin of the world.

2. God knew all about us before he saved us. He knew all the sins we would ever commit. Yet he saved us just the same. When the Lord Jesus died, he died for all our sins—past, present, and future. Actually, when he died they were all future—and he died for them all. Therefore, the penalty for all these sins has been paid once. God will not demand payment twice—first at the hands of Christ, and then at the hands of the believer. This would be unjust, and God could not act unjustly.

3. As we have seen before, salvation is a gift. God does not give one day and take back the next. "The gifts and calling of God are irrevocable" (Romans 11:29 NKJV).

4. Salvation is spoken of as a birth (John 3:3). When a person is saved, he is born from above. He then becomes a child of God (John 1:12). Now a birth is final and unchangeable. Once it has taken place, it can never be undone. A child may grieve or even disgrace his father, but the relationship still exists.

So it is with the new birth. A Christian may sin and grieve the heart of God, but God is still his Father. This is clearly stated in 1 John 2:1: "And if any man sin, we have an advocate with the Father." He is still our Father, even if we sin.

Sin breaks *fellowship* with God, but not *relationship.*

5. A believer is no more able to keep himself saved than he was to save himself in the first place. When the Galatians attempted to do this, Paul asked them:

Are you so foolish? Having begun in the Spirit, are you now being made perfect by the flesh? (Galatians 3:3 NKJV).

6. God has paid too dearly for his people to ever give them up. He saved us when we were his enemies. Will he abandon us now when we are his children?

If when we were enemies we were reconciled to God through the death of His Son, much more, having been reconciled, we shall be saved by His life (Romans 5:10 NKJV).

7. God promises *eternal* life to the believer. How long is *eternal?* It is forever. "I give unto them *eternal* life, and they shall never perish" (John 10:28; see also John 3:16, 36; 6:47). He will never go back on his promise.

8. The Holy Spirit of God is said to indwell the believer forever. "He will give you another Helper, that He may abide with you forever" (John 14:16–17; see also 1 John 2:27).

9. The believer is also said to be sealed by the Holy Spirit unto the day of redemption (Ephesians 4:30). And the Holy Spirit is the "guarantee of our inheritance until the redemption of the purchased possession" (Ephesians 1:14 NKJV). This guarantees his ministry for the child of God until heaven is reached at last.

From the above, it should be evident that the Christian is "kept by the power of God through faith unto salvation ready to be revealed in the last time" (1 Peter 1:5).

THE TRUE MEANING OF GRACE

To say that this is a dangerous doctrine is to show a

decided lack of appreciation for the meaning of grace. Also, it creates the fantastic idea that whenever a person is saved, he immediately has a strong urge to commit fornication, murder, and other vile sins, and that unless he is restrained by fear of punishment, he will actually do these things. What are the facts? The facts are these:

a. Instead of encouraging men to sin, the doctrine of eternal security presents the strongest reason why men should not sin. The knowledge that God has provided a full, free, and eternal salvation makes the believer want to serve him forever.

Love is a stronger force than fear of punishment. Men will do, out of a sense of love, what they would never do through fear. Love binds the heart like nothing else does.

> It is not necessary that men should be kept in continual dread of damnation to render them circumspect. Love is the noblest and strongest principle of obedience: a sense of God's love to us will increase our desire to please Him (Robinson).

Therefore, the Christian does not live a holy life in order to retain his salvation, but through love to the One who saved him. To him, it is a greater crime to sin against grace than against law.

b. Second, when a person is saved, he receives a new nature (2 Peter 1:4). Instead of having a strong urge to sin, the Christian has a hatred of sin that he never had before.

This new nature not only creates a horror of sin but causes the believer to be most miserable when he does sin. To have one's fellowship with the Father broken is one of the worst tragedies of the Christian life. It is to experience shame for indulging in that which caused the death of our Savior. It is to experience the chastisement of a loving heavenly Father. It is to experience loss of reward at the Judgment Seat of Christ (1 Corinthians 3:15). Not until the erring Christian confesses and forsakes that sin is he restored to the full fellowship of his Lord.

Of course, a man may profess to be saved and then go out and live in sin. It is not just that he commits occasional acts of sin, but he practices sin. It is the habit of his life. Here it is not a matter of the person's having been saved and then lost. This man proves by his behavior that he never was genuinely saved at all. He is merely a false professor who has never truly experienced the grace of God.

But for those who have genuinely trusted the living, loving Savior, there is the unfailing promise of God that he will take them safely home to heaven. They can sing with the utmost confidence:

> *My name from the palms of His hands,*
> *Eternity will not erase;*
> *Imprest on His heart it remains,*
> *In marks of indelible grace.*
> *Yes, I to the end shall endure,*
> *As sure as the earnest is given,*
> *More happy but not more secure,*
> *The souls of the blessed in heaven.*

9

*F*eelings or Facts?

How May You Know You Are Saved?

It is not uncommon for one who has believed on the Lord Jesus Christ to have serious doubts afterward as to whether he was really saved. He expected some mysterious spectacular experience, but in his particular case there was none. He expected that there would be no more strivings with sin; but instead of that, he finds that these have actually seemed to increase. Thus he becomes discouraged and wonders how he can know for sure whether he is saved.

*W*HAT DOES THE BIBLE SAY?

By a series of questions, we can illustrate how one who has cried to God for salvation may know that he is saved:

Is the Bible the Word of God? (2 Timothy 3: 16–17).

Is God true to his Word? (Matthew 5:18).

Has God promised to save all those who call upon him? (Romans 10:13).

Will God save a sinner who believes on the Lord Jesus Christ? (Acts 16:31; Romans 10:9).

HAVE YOU BELIEVED IN CHRIST?

Have you ever confessed to God that you are a sinner and asked him to save you on the basis of what Christ did for you as your substitute?

If you can sincerely and honestly answer "Yes" to all these questions, we ask, "Are you saved?"

The only sensible answer is, "Of course I am saved. God, who cannot lie, promises to save me if I trust his Son. I have accepted the Savior, and therefore I am saved. God's Word says so" (1 John 5:13).

> For this reason I also suffer these things; nevertheless I am not ashamed, for I know whom I have believed and am persuaded that He is able to keep what I have committed to Him against that Day (2 Timothy 1:12 NKJV).

No one has ever come to God as a sinner, asked for salvation in the name of the Lord Jesus, and been refused (John 6:37).

WHICH WILL YOU TRUST?
THE BIBLE OR YOUR FEELINGS?

But the trouble is that people look to their feelings rather than to the Bible. The Bible says, in effect, "All who believe in Christ are saved." But they say, "I don't feel saved. Surely if I were truly saved I shouldn't be troubled by doubts, fears, temptations, and anxieties. I felt saved yesterday but I don't feel saved today." They doubt the Bible and trust their feelings.

When the thief on the cross beside the Savior heard him say, "Today you will be with Me in Paradise" (Luke 23:43 NKJV), how did he know he was saved? Was it by his feelings? No, his feelings at that moment were anything but encouraging. He knew he was saved because the Lord Jesus said so. That is how we know we are saved; we hear his voice telling us, not audibly, but through the written Word.

> *He does not make the soul to say,*
> *"Thank God, I feel so good,"*
> *But turns the eye another way*
> *To Jesus and His Word.*

It is impossible for you to "feel" saved until you take God at his Word. Then you *know* you are saved.

A BIBLICAL ILLUSTRATION

In Old Testament times, when God determined to redeem the nation of Israel from its bondage in the land of Egypt, he sent Moses as his ambassador. Because Pharaoh refused to obey Moses, God decided on one final step. He would judge Pharaoh and all Egypt in such a way that Pharaoh would not dare to trifle further. On an appointed night God would send an angel to slay every firstborn male in Egypt. A way of escape, however, was provided.

The angel would pass over any household that took the simple steps of salvation God outlined (see Exodus 12).

1. Each family must take a lamb, perfect and without blemish. The lamb must be kept for four days, then slain and its blood caught in a basin.

2. Next the blood must be applied to the framework of the door of each house.

3. The family, including the doomed firstborn, must take shelter in the house behind the blood-splashed entrance.

4. If this were done, the firstborn would be safe.

George Cutting, in his little booklet, *Safety, Certainty and Enjoyment,* uses this Old Testament incident to illustrate how we can know that we are saved.

He says: How did the firstborn sons of the thousands of Israel know for certain that they were safe the night of the Passover and Egypt's judgment?

Let us visit two of their houses and hear what they have to say. In the first house they are all shivering with fear and suspense. We ask them why. The firstborn son informs us that the angel of death is coming through the land and that he is not quite certain how matters will stand with him at the solemn moment.

"When the destroying angel has passed our house," he says, "and the night of judgment is over. I shall then know that I am safe; but I can't see how I can be quite sure of it until then. They say they are sure of salvation next door, but we think it very presumptuous. All I can do is spend the night hoping for the best."

"Well," we inquire, "has the God of Israel not provided a way of safety for his people?"

"Oh yes," he replies, "and we have availed ourselves of that way of escape. The blood of the spotless and unblemished first-year lamb has been duly sprinkled with the bunch of hyssop on the lintel and two side posts, but we still are not fully assured of shelter."

Let us now leave these and enter the house next door. What a striking contrast! Peace rests on every countenance. There they stand, with girded loins and with staff at hand, feeding on the roasted lamb.

We ask, "How can you have such peace on such a solemn night as this?"

"Ah," they say, "we are only waiting for Jehovah's marching order. Then we shall bid a last farewell to this hateful land of bondage."

"Are you forgetting that this is the night of Egypt's judgment?"

"No; but our firstborn is safe. The blood has been sprinkled according to the wish of our God."

"So it has been next door," we reply, "but they are all unhappy because they are uncertain of safety."

"Ah," firmly responds the firstborn, "but we have more than the sprinkled blood. We have the unerring Word of God about it. God has said, 'When I see the blood, I will pass over you.' God rests satisfied with the blood outside, and we rest satisfied with his Word inside."

You see the sprinkled blood makes us safe. The spoken Word makes us sure. Could anything make us more safe than the sprinkled blood, or more sure than his spoken Word? Nothing!

Now, then, let me ask you a question. Which of those two houses was the safer? Do you say the second, where all were so peaceful? Then you are wrong. *Both are safe alike.* Their safety depends upon what God thinks about the blood outside and not upon the state of their feelings inside.

If you would be sure of your own blessings, then listen not to the unstable testimony of inward emotions but to the infallible witness of the Word of God.

"Most assuredly, I say unto you, he who believes on Me has everlasting life" (John 6:47 NKJV).

ANOTHER ILLUSTRATION

George Cutting tells also of a farmer who, not having sufficient grass for his cattle, asks a local landowner to sell him some property. For some time he gets no answer from the owner.

One day a neighbor comes in and says, "I feel quite sure you will get that field. Don't you remember that last Christmas the owner sent you a present and that he gave you a nod of recognition the other day when he drove past?" And with such words the farmer's mind is filled with hope.

Next day another neighbor meets him, and in course of conversation he says, "I'm afraid you will stand no chance whatever of getting that field. Mr. Jones has applied for it, and you know what a favorite he is with the owner." And the poor farmer's bright hopes are gone. One day he is hopeful, the next day full of perplexing doubts.

Presently the mailman comes, and the farmer anxiously opens the letter because it is from the owner himself. See his countenance change from suspense to joy as he reads and rereads that letter.

"It's settled now!" He exclaims to his wife. No more doubts and fears about it. Hopes and ifs are part of the past. "The owner says the field is mine, and that's enough for me. His word settles it."

Many people are in a similar condition—tossed and

perplexed by the opinions of men or by the thoughts and feelings of their own hearts. It is only upon receiving the Word of God that certainty takes the place of doubts.

TWO ADDITIONAL PROOFS OF THE NEW BIRTH

Although assurance of salvation comes first and principally by believing what God has said, it is not the only proof of the new birth. Two others are as follows:

1. *The witness of the Holy Spirit.* "The Spirit Himself bears witness with our spirit that we are the children of God" (Romans 8:16 NKJV). The Spirit witnesses through the Scriptures. When a believer reads the promise of God and believes it, the Holy Spirit fills him with joy and peace. Then in his prayer life, his worship, and his service, the Christian becomes conscious of the working of the Spirit of God.

2. *The change in one's life and ways.* For instance, a Christian knows he has passed from death to life because he now loves others (1 John 3:14). Also, there is a changed attitude toward sin. The believer hates sin and is ashamed of himself when he permits himself to sin.

If there is no change in a person's life or behavior, it is doubtful that he ever was saved. That is what James meant when he said so pointedly, "Faith without works is dead" (James 2:20). It is useless for a man to say that he has faith if that faith does not result in good works. The faith that saves is the faith that works—that changes the pattern of one's behavior.

TO DOUBT GOD IS SIN!

Do not doubt God. He says that those who believe on

Christ are saved. To disbelieve this is to make God a liar (1 John 5:10). It is not humility to refuse his Word. It is sin. No matter what your feelings may be, God's Word is true and must be trusted. "Forever, O LORD, Your Word is settled in heaven" (Psalm 119:89 NKJV).

George Cutting illustrates this truth, too, with the following personal illustration.

> "I do really believe on him," said a young person to me one day, "but yet, when asked if I am saved, I don't like to say yes, for fear I would be telling a lie."
>
> This young woman was a butcher's daughter in a small town. Each week her father went to the stockyards to buy his meat, and the day the conversation took place happened to be the day he went. So I said, "Now suppose when your father comes home you ask him how many sheep he bought today?" and he replies, "I don't like to say, for fear I should be telling a lie.'"
>
> "But," said the mother (who was standing by at the time), "that would be making her father a liar."
>
> Don't you see that this well-meaning young woman was virtually making Christ out to be a liar? She was saying, "I do believe on the Son of God, and he says I have everlasting life, but I don't like to say I have it for fear I should be telling a lie."

10

The Christian Life

The Christian's Standing and State

The Christian's position is perfect. God sees him in Christ—holy and unblamable (Ephesians 1:4). But the Christian is still troubled by three enemies—the world (1 John 2:15–16), the flesh (Romans 7:18), and the devil (1 Peter 5:8). Often, therefore, his practice is that of weakness and failure (Matthew 26:41).

The Christian's *standing* depends on the work of Christ, and that is why it is perfect. However, his *state* depends upon his own walk, and that is why it is often far from perfect.

God can look upon the believer as absolutely faultless because Christ has borne the penalty of his sins. The believer need never worry about being condemned eternally for his sins, because the price has been paid for all his sins—past, present, and future (Hebrews 10:17; Psalm 103:12).

> *God will not payment twice demand,*
> *First at my Saviour's pierced hand*
> *And then again at mine.*

JUDICIAL CONDEMNATION AND PARENTAL DISCIPLINE

But does that mean that God can overlook sins committed after a person is saved? No, it does not. God can never be indifferent to sin. However, there is a difference between punishing a criminal and chastening a child. We have already seen that the punishment of our sins was endured by the sinless substitute—the Lord Jesus; so that the Christian will not be sent to hell for them. What, then, happens when a Christian does sin? Simply this. Sin in the life of the believer breaks fellowship with God. The happy atmosphere of the household is gone. God must now treat the disobedient one as a father would treat an erring child (Hebrews 12:5–9). The child must be lovingly disciplined until he confesses his sin and forsakes it (1 John 1:9). The backslider must be corrected and restored to the Lord. In extreme cases, God even chastens his child with physical death (1 Corinthians 5:5; 11:30; 1 John 5:16).

There is a difference between judicial condemnation and parental discipline. The judge on the bench condemns the lawbreaker, requiring him to pay the penalty for his deed. But when the same judge goes home and finds that his son has been disobedient, does he condemn him to go to prison or to pay a fine? No, he simply chastens him with a view to restoring him to the enjoyment of his place in the family.

In the same way, God judged the believer's sins at Calvary; the believer died in the person of Christ. But now that he is God's child, the Father lovingly chastens him when he wanders away.

GOD SAYS TO THE CHRISTIAN: "GROW IN GRACE"

God desires our state to become increasingly like our standing. He does not want us to sin (1 John 2:1). He has said to us, in effect, You are perfect (Hebrews 10:14), now be perfect (Matthew 5:48). You are saved (John 3:16), now work out your salvation (Philippians 2:12).

Actually, the child of God will not be free from sin entirely until the Savior comes and takes him home to heaven. But during his lifetime, he can and should grow in grace by prayer, Bible study, and meditation—becoming more and more like the Lord Jesus (2 Peter 3:18).

WALK WORTHILY OF THE CALLING

The uniform teaching of the New Testament with regard to the Christian life is that believers should walk in a manner that is consistent with their high calling (Ephesians 4:1–3). One of the outstanding passages on this theme is Titus 2:11–14 (NKJV):

> For the grace of God that brings salvation has appeared to all men, teaching us that, denying ungodliness and worldly lusts, we should live soberly, righteously, and godly in the present age, looking for

the blessed hope and glorious appearing of our great
God and Savior Jesus Christ, who gave Himself for us,
that He might redeem us from every lawless deed and
purify for Himself His own special people, zealous for
good works.

There is a fable about a crow who wished to join a company of doves. He realized that his black feathers were a handicap so he rolled in a heap of white ashes to lighten their hue. But the doves backed away from him.

Thinking things over, the crow decided that the doves could see that his walk was different from theirs. They walked; he hopped. So he practiced putting one foot down after the other until he acquired a fair imitation of their walk, and again he tried to join the doves. Still they would have nothing to do with him.

This time the crow decided it was because he liked to eat flesh whereas the doves preferred grain, so he determined to change his eating habits. In time he was able to persuade the doves that he was one of them; but just as he was enjoying his success, another crow flew overhead and, recognizing the crow among the doves, let out a loud "Caw!" Forgetting himself for a moment the crow replied in like fashion.

That was the end! Never again could the crow find his fellowship with the doves. His *walk* was different; his *food* was different, and his *talk* was different.

The true Christian is marked out from a person of the world by these same three traits. His walk is with God, his food is God's Word, and his talk is clean and Christ-exalting.

A missionary used to tell the following story about an Indian who came to one of their mission stations desiring to be a Christian.

"I have been a warrior," the Indian said, "and my hands are stained with blood. Could I be a Christian?"

The Indian was pointed to the Savior and told that God loved him and that Christ died for him.

At once the Indian professed faith in Christ. To test him the missionary said, "May I cut your hair?"

The Indians, of course, wore their scalp-lock for their enemies. When it was cut, it was a sign that they would never go on the warpath again.

The Indian said, "Yes, you may cut it. I shall throw my old life away."

It was cut, and the converted Indian left for home. On the way he met some of his old companions who shouted with laughter.

"Yesterday," they taunted, "you were a brave, today you are a squaw."

The Indian was stung to madness. Rushing to his home he threw himself on the floor and burst into tears. His wife, a Christian, came to him and said, "Yesterday there was not a man in the world who dared to call you a coward. Can't you be as brave for him who died for you as you were to kill the Sioux?"

He instantly sprang to his feet and said, "I can and I will."

"I have known many brave, fearless servants of Christ," said the missionary, "but I never knew one braver than this chief."

A GODLY LIFE: THE FRUIT OF— NOT THE MEANS TO—SALVATION

Notice carefully this important distinction: a believer

does not lead a good life in order to become a Christian. Rather he aims to please the Lord by a life of holiness because he is a Christian (Romans 6:1–2).

> *I would not work my soul to save;*
> *This work my Lord hath done.*
> *But I would work like any slave,*
> *For love to God's dear Son.*

This is the difference between law and grace. Law says: "If you live a godly, sinless life, you will be safe. If not, you will perish forever in hell."

Grace says: "Since you cannot live without sinning, therefore, it is true that you are cursed. But—God sent his Son to die in your place. If you receive him by faith, you are saved. Then out of love to him, you should seek to please him in all that you say and do. You should "reckon yourselves dead indeed unto sin, but alive unto God through Jesus Christ our Lord" (Romans 6:11).

Love is the strongest of all motives, and sinners saved by grace are impelled by that motive to live in separation from sin and the world that crucified God's Son.

11

The Great Choice

Knowledge Is Not Faith

It is tragically possible that a person may know all the facts presented in this book and still not be saved. The miracle of the new birth does not take place when a person is informed of certain great Bible doctrines. If that were the case, then the task of the evangelist would be simply that of education.

But that is not the gospel at all!

It is a Person to be received (John 1:12). The Lord Jesus Christ is the only one who can save.

It is a gift to be taken. "The gift of God is eternal life through Jesus Christ our Lord" (Romans 6:23).

A person knows whether or not he has ever made this

vital decision. He knows if there was ever a time in his life when eternal issues weighed heavily on him; when the burden of his sins seemed intolerable; and when, by a simple act of faith, he confessed his sins and believed on the Lord Jesus Christ.

BE RECONCILED TO GOD

In the event that you have never done it, this is the question of all questions: Will you do it now? Will you come as a repentant sinner to the Son of God, and crown him as your Lord and Savior? Will you commit yourself to him? "Now then, we are ambassadors for Christ, as though God were pleading through us, we implore you on Christ's behalf, be reconciled to God" (2 Corinthians 5:20 NKJV).

You can do it while you are studying this book. Without any outward sign, you can bow your head, tell God that you are a sinner, receive Christ as your Savior, and accept the gift of eternal life. Upon the authority of God's infallible Word, you will be saved the moment you do this.

The act of believing on Christ is illustrated by the marriage ceremony. The bride is asked, "Do you take this man to be your lawful, wedded husband . . . ?" She answers, "I do." In saying this she accepts a person and commits herself to him. In believing on Christ, we accept him as our only Lord and Savior and commit ourselves to him for this life and for eternity.

Jesus likened salvation to entering a door. "I am the door: by me if any man enter in he shall be saved" (John 10:9).

When we sit on a chair, we rest our weight on the finished work of the furniture manufacturer. When we believe on Christ, we rest on his finished work as the sole and sufficient price of our redemption.

This is the time for you to decide. You may never have another opportunity. Forget your excuses. Refuse to be turned aside. Without further hesitation, open your heart's door and let the Savior in.

> Behold I stand at the door and knock: if any man hear my voice, and open the door, I will come in to him, and will sup with him, and he with me (Revelation 3:20).

THANK GOD FOR SAVING YOU

After you have opened the door of your heart to Christ, the first thing you should do is thank him for saving you (Luke 17:15–16). This unique gift should not be accepted without a grateful response. Your thanksgiving does not need to be elegant. If it comes from the heart, it will be pleasing to God (Psalms 50:23).

CONFESS CHRIST OPENLY

A second thing you should do is to confess Christ openly to others (Romans 10:9). It was the Savior himself who said:

> Whoever confesses Me before men, him I will also confess before My Father who is in heaven (Matthew 10:32 NKJV).

Tell others that you are a child of God by faith in Jesus Christ.

85

STUDY THE BIBLE AND PRAY

Third, spend time each day in feeding on the Word of God and in prayer (2 Timothy 2:15; 1 Timothy 2:1–4). This is absolutely essential for growth (1 Peter 2:2), for holiness (Psalm 119:7, 11) and for effective service (Ephesians 6:17).

SEEK FELLOWSHIP WITH OTHER CHRISTIANS

Another great benefit in the Christian life is fellowship with other believers. A Bible-believing church, where Christ is recognized as head and where everything is tested by the Word of God (Isaiah 8:20), should be attended regularly (Hebrews 10:25).

LEAD SINNERS TO THE SAVIOR

Paul exhorted young Timothy:

> The things that you have heard from me among many witnesses, commit them to faithful men who will be able to teach others also (2 Timothy 2:2 NKJV).

This is God's way of spreading the Christian faith. Not every believer can preach from a pulpit; but everyone can tell his unsaved relatives, neighbors, and friends what thrilling things the Lord has done for him (Mark 5:19).

ENTHRONE JESUS AS LORD OF YOUR LIFE

Above all, the Savior should be crowned as Lord of your life (Romans 12:1–2). You received him as Lord; he should continue to hold this place. This should not need emphasis. You should reckon that, if he went to such unparalleled cost to save you, then surely he deserves everything that you have and are. This was in the apostle Paul's mind when he said:

> For the love of Christ compels us, because we judge thus: that if One died for all, then all died; and He died for all, that those who live should live no longer for themselves, but for Him who died for them and rose again (2 Corinthians 5:14–15 NKJV).

The famous missionary, C.T. Studd, said, "If Jesus Christ be God and died for me, then no sacrifice can be too great for me to make for him." The only logical, reasonable action for you is to turn over complete control of your life to the one who bought you (1 Corinthians 6:20) and to say to him:

> *O Christ, Thy bleeding hands and feet,*
> *Thy sacrifice for me,*
> *Each wound, each tear, demand my life,*
> *A sacrifice for Thee.*